MY FIRST NUMBERS

CHILDHOOD TRAUMA

VOLUME ONE

T. C. DOWNER

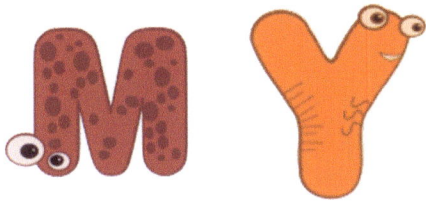

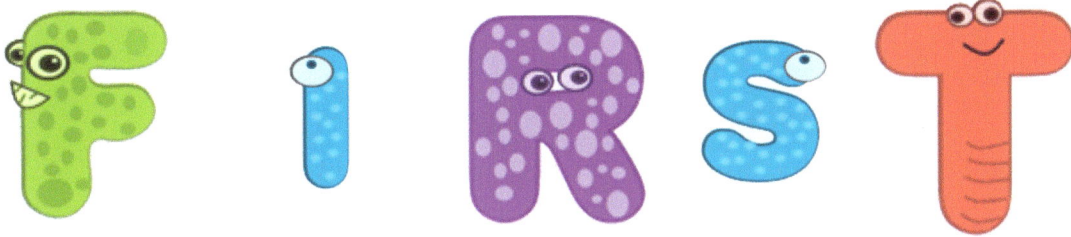

MY FIRST NUMBERS

BY T. C. DOWNER

To a good sense of humor

The number of times mommy remembered your birthday.

The number of times daddy showers each week.

The number of abortions mommy had before you were born.

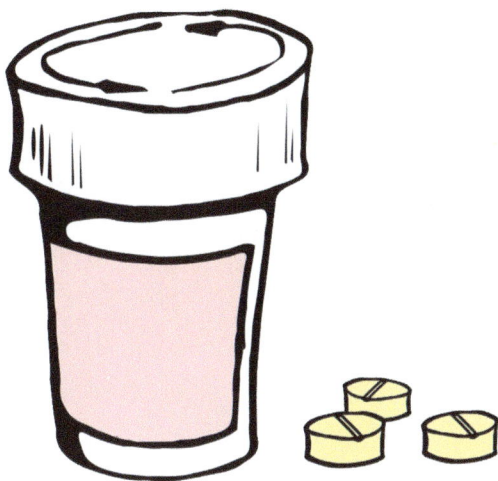

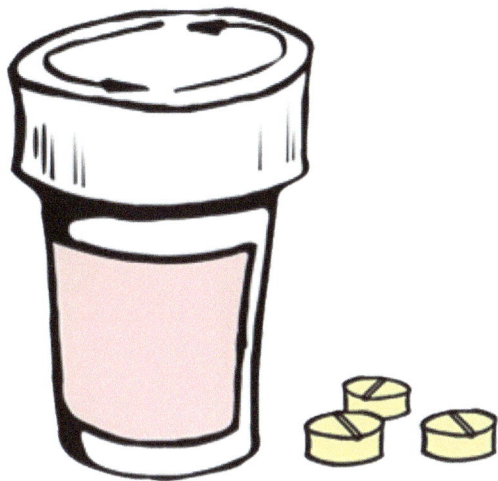

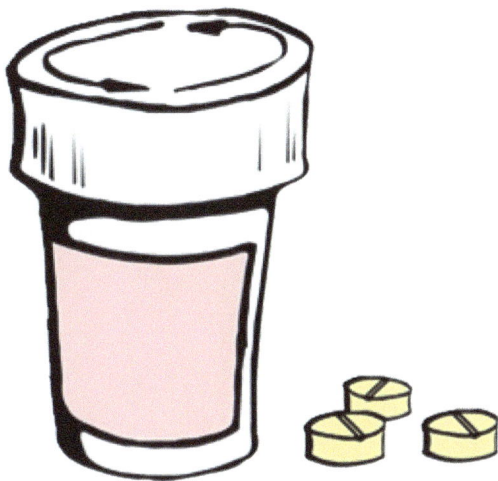

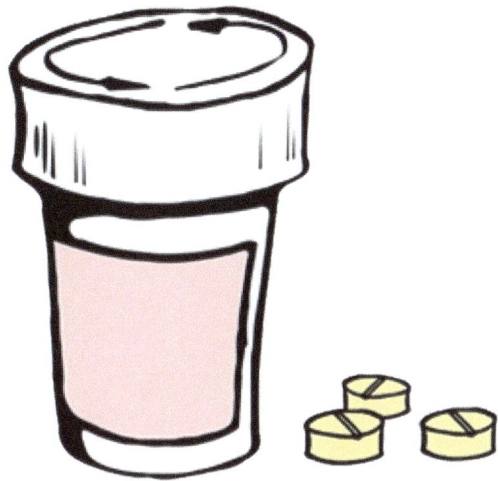

The number of sexually transmitted diseases your daddy has caught.

The number of alcoholic drinks mommy has after work.

The number of hours daddy left you alone in the car.

The number of days mommy and daddy smoke marijuana each week.

The number of times daddy hired a prostitute.

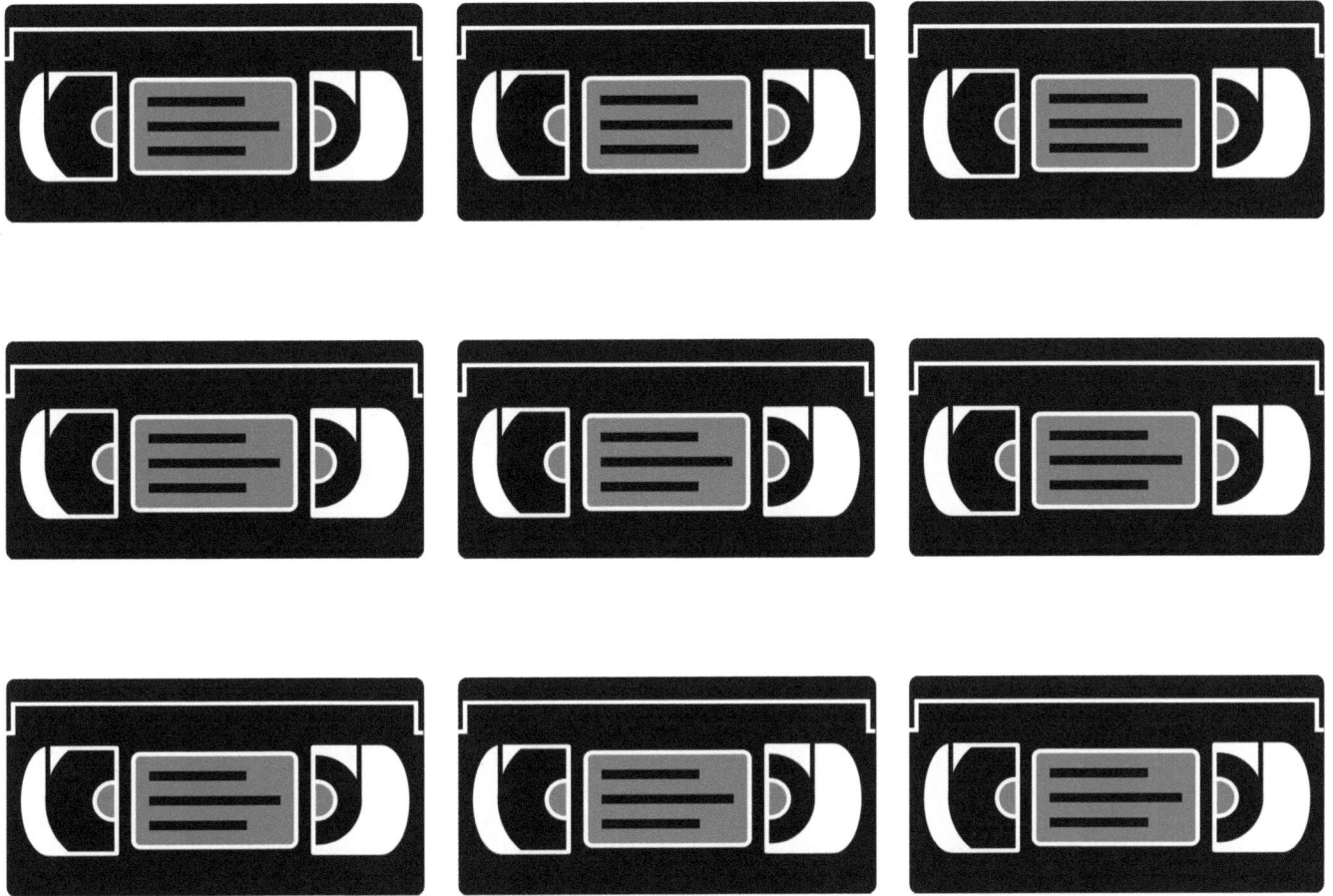

The number of pornographic videos your mommy has been in.

The number of children mommy and daddy wish they had.

www.ingramcontent.com/pod-product-compliance
Lightning Source LLC
Chambersburg PA
CBHW041556040426
42447CB00002B/193